THE ALL NEW STYLE OF MAGAZINE-BOOKS

SDM LIVE ®

www.SDMLIVE.com

MP

MOCY PUBLISHING
WWW.MOCYPUBLISHING.COM

SDM LIVE®

EDITOR-IN-CHIEF
D. "Casino" Bailey
casino@sdmlive.com

EDITORIAL DIRECTOR
Sheree Cranford
sheree@sdmlive.com

GRAPHIC/WEB DESIGNER
D. "Casino" Bailey
casino@sdmlive.com

ACCOUNT EXECUTIVE
Frank Harvest Jr.
frank@sdmlive.com

PHOTOGRAPHERS
Anterlon Terrell Fritz
Treagen Colston
Terance Drake

CONTRIBUTORS
April Smiley
Courtney Benjamin

COPY ORDERS & ADVERTISING OFFICE
Send Money Order or Check to:
Mocy Publishing
P.O. Box 35195
Detroit, Michigan 48235
(586) 646-8505
advertise@sdmlive.com

Copy Order Item
SDM Live Magazine Issue #16
S&H Plus Retail Price - $9.99 per copy

WWW.SDMLIVE.COM

Printed by CreateSpace, An Amazon.com Company

MOCY PUBLISHING

REAL MUSIC. REAL ENTERTAINMENT.®
SDM LIVE
ISSUE 16

ALSO
AVA
VERDICT
N.O.V.A.
J FOCUZ
SHAWNY
R.G.S.

NEW

LISA SPATES
THE FASHION DESIGNER OF SOFLUFFY CREATIONS IS PUTTING KIDS CLOTHING BACK ON THE PUBLIC RADOR

DJ STEADY ROCK
MR. CHENE PARK IS GEARING UP FOR THE SUMMER OF 2017

WWW.SDMLIVE.COM

ISSUE 16 - 2017
CONTENTS

pg. 12
DJ STEADY ROCK

The hottest DJ and mixer on the airwaves and turn tables.

pg. 16
LISA SPATES

Designing for kids, fashion shows, events, birthdays, holidays, and more.

pg. 20
THE SHOWCASE

Royalty Gang Records has presented another I love music showcase.

pg. 23
TOP 10 CHARTS

The hottest albums and digital singles this month features Tee Grizzley, Rick Ross, Kendrick Lamar and more.

1

iRobot - Roomba 650 Self-Charging Robot Vacuum - Black
$299.99
www.bestbuy.com

2

GoPro - HERO5 Black 4K Action Camera
$399.99
www.bestbuy.com

3

Dell - Inspiron 23.8" Touch-Screen All-In-One - Intel Core i7 - 12GB Memory - 1TB Hard Drive - Silver
$999.99
www.bestbuy.com

Life is Why We Walk

SDMLIVE RADIO SHOWS ITS COMMUNITY SUPPORT AS THE COMPANY PREPARES FOR THE 2017 ANNUAL AMERICAN HEART ASSOCIATION WALK

by Cheraee C.

Both heart disease and stroke are critical and global epidemics, but thanks to organizations like the American Heart Association for saving lives every day. The AHA has been rounding up its donors, walkers, and runners all over the United States. The AHA's next stop is on May 20th downtown Detroit at Wayne State University at 8am sharp.

SDMLive is proud to announce we will be participating in the heart walk and we invite all of our supporters to walk with us. The AHA's goal is to make 1,600,000 and that's just their Detroit stats. With all the businesses and entreprenuer we have in Detroit it should be no reason why we can't surpass this goal. Get your water bottles, your jogging pants, and your walking shoes ready for the annual heart walk and make a small donation to help save a life!

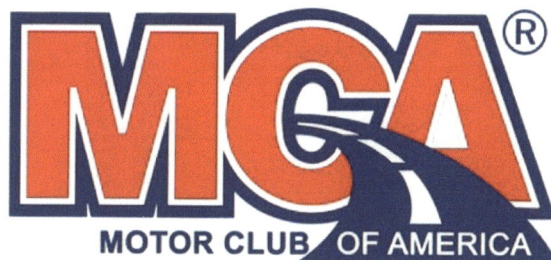

Crude Affiliation

URBAN FICTION WRITER AND DETROIT NATIVE LL MARIE GETS NITTY AND GRITTY WITH HER NEW BOOK RELEASE

by Cheraee C.

Detroit's own LL Marie was on a literary mission when she wrote her debut novel Crude Affiliation: When The Choice Isn't Yours. You never know what different affiliations can lead you too.

This 617 page urban thriller is super descriptive from the first sentence to the last chapter. Each and every memory, experience, and scene is expressed to the fullest extent showing realism and symbolism. If you don't know anything about Detroit or want to know what it's like to come up in Detroit you will after reading this book.

As a mother and her five sons Ray, Sway, Cent, Ronnie, and Lester each highlight their lives from boy to men, from the streets to the sheets, you are in for a page-turning journey.

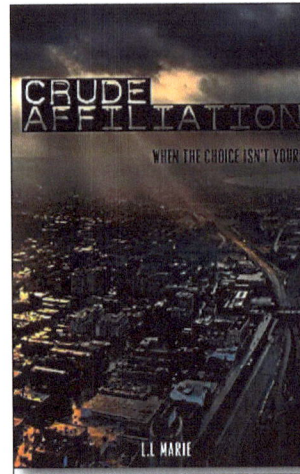

Crude Affiliation: When The Choice Isn't Yours
By LL Marie

Available from Amazon.com and other online stores

COMING SOON!!!

A BOOK OF SHORT STORIES & POETRY

Brown Paper Suga

forwarded by
Cheraee C.

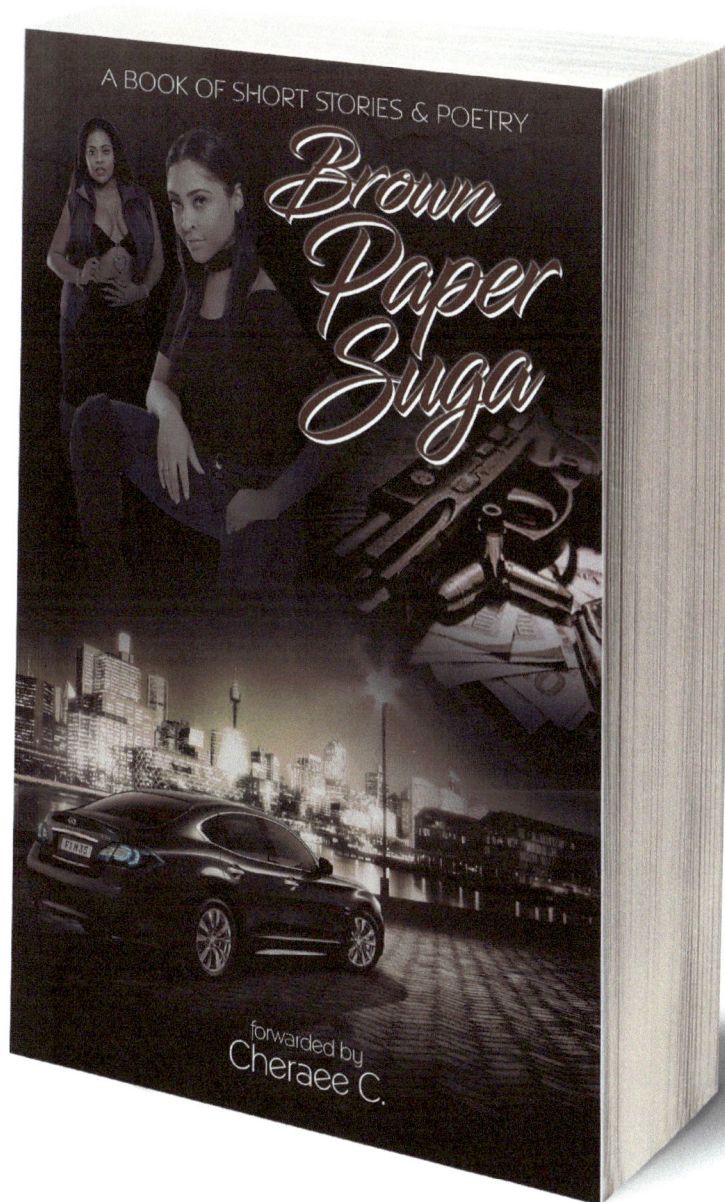

Brown Paper Suga
By Cheraee C.

He Still Steady Rocking

DJ STEADY ROCK HAS MANY GOALS AS HE DJS FOR THE HOTTEST CORPORATE EVENTS, WEDDINGS, SHOWS, CONCERTS, AND ON HOT 107.5

by Cheraee C.

Q. How'd you get the nickname Mr. Chene Park?

A. I actually got the name Mr. Chene Park from Dr. Darrius. I have been dejaying concerts at Chene Park since 2003, and one day me and Dr. Darrius was on air together and he was like "Mr. Chene Park in da building!!" I have embraced it ever since and I would like to s/o to Sulaiman Mausi and the Mausi family for having me there for the past 14yrs.

Q. How'd you get the opportunity to start dejaying on the radio at Hot 107.5?

A. I started in radio in 2001, winning a spot to be a mixer on WJLB FM 98. After 7yrs there, I departed the radio station and was the DJ on the TV Show, "Dance Party", on WADL. After just 1 month, I became the host and the DJ of that show. After changes at the TV station, 2 yrs later, the PD (Jay Hicks at the time) at Hot 107.5 gave me a shot to mix on the station in 2011 and I have been there since then.

Q. Is there any type of event you don't DJ at and why?

A. Hmmm, I would have to say yard parties in the city unless it's someone I know personally for safety reasons.

Q. How did you meet PDot and become her official DJ?

A. I met P-Dot when she performed at an "Imported From Tha D" Showcase at St. Andrews. Roughly around six months later, we ran into each other and had a conversation about her not having a DJ, and made it official.

Q. What is your opinion of all these DJs out here, people who just slap DJ in front of their name and buy DJ equipment?

A. Let's just say I can't knock nobody's hustle, lol, but having equipment and a laptop and a few music files DO NOT make you a DJ. For me a DJ has the passion for music and entertaining people. I'm more than just a DJ, I consider myself an entertainer. It's not just a job, for me it's a lifestyle.

Q. Are you apart of any of the DJ groups in Detroit? Street Hitta Djs? Coalition DJs? Which group why or why not?

A. No, currently I'm not in a DJ group out of Detroit, even though I am good friends with Bigg Dawg Blast, CEO of Street Hitta DJ's. I am, however, in the nationwide Core DJ's under the CEO Tony Neal. Nothing against the Detroit DJ crews, but here I choose to focus on my own brand, DJ Stead Rock Entertainment.

Q. What events or projects do you have lined up for this summer?

A. Just like every summer, of course I will be at Chene Park, lol, clubs, concerts, and corporate events. I also travel and do events with a well known painter named Patcasso. No matter how big or how small the event is, I don't discriminate, entertainment is my life!

Nova The Bully

THE B.U.L.L.Y BRAND C.E.O IS TEACHING EVERYONE TO BE UNAFRAID AND LEARN TO LOVE YOURSELF AS HE BECOMES A HOUSEHOLD NAME
by Cheraee C.

Q. What are two things you currently dislike about the underground music scene and why?

A. Well number one is the lack of unity. Everyone is against everyone. I wish we realized that if we unify we can get more accomplished. We all have the same goal to be heard and become successful, and to provide for our families. And the second would be the lack of originality. We have so many artists here in Detroit that tries to sound like other artists. We have too much talent here I feel we need to step out of the box and be in your own lane.

Q. What is the craziest experience you had at a video shoot?

A. The craziest experience was when I shot a video at the old packard plant in Detroit. At first I was skeptical because it looked like a scene from a horror film, but this particular day the security was not letting us get nothing done. They kept interrupting telling us we needed permits to shoot. But we eventually got it done, and it turned out to be a dope video.

Q. How do you feel about your music career thus far?

A. Honestly it's been a long journey filled with ups and downs. I love the fact that people are finally starting to take notice, it keeps me going, Plus it helps that I make the kind of music I like to make even though it can be dark it's my therapy.

Q. If a major music producer came up to you right now and offered you a deal, what would you say, what would you do?

A. Well all deals aren't good deals, but I would definitely listen, and if it makes Dollars as well as Sense than why not as long as I can negotiate some of my own terms I'm sure we could reach an agreement.

Q. What are your major goals for your music career in 2017?

A. For Nova The Bully to be a household name and help bring awareness to my brand the B.U.L.L.Y Brand which is an acronym that means Be Unafraid Learn to Love Yourself. As well as make my music company Business and No Games LLC one of the hottest labels with some of the dopest, most well-rounded artists that anyone has ever seen. #BANG

We Have The Verdict

STRAIGHT FROM EAST COLLEGE ST., VERDICT IS PREPARING FOR HIS UPCOMING PROJEC T AND BUILDING HIS BRAND BENOFFICAL MUSIC

by: Cheraee C.

Q. What is the title of your latest project and describe the meaning behind it.

A. I have a project set to be released sometime in May (hopefully.) It is titled "College Ain't For Everybody." The meaning behind the title actually depends on whom you are to me and how YOU the listener sees it. One of the meanings are a representation of the street that I was raised on which is named College street. Another would be based off the last project I released which is loosely based off of Lean On Me the movie, but throughout the album I incorporate my upbringing on the Eastside of Detroit. So rightfully after high school is college, but with the career I have college isn't a necessity, but with the neighborhood I'm from college would be perfect escape, but it ain't for everybody. Makes sense?

Q. Do you feel like you take a political/realistic stance in your music and why?

A. I honestly feel in my music I deliver my life and my world as I see and feel it. I wouldn't consider myself a political artist though. If I touch on a social topic it's more than likely because it affected me mentally. Now don't get me wrong there are things that happen and I feel like concerned about it, but I don't address it musically.

Q. What's one of your past experiences you never expressed in your music, but want too?

A. Oooh. Um let me think there was this one time at band camp lol, but seriously I can't think of one. I've discussed everything in my music from my children's birth, my self-doubt at times, being paranoid, you name it if it's happened to me I spoke on it.

Q. What are some of your hobbies other than music?

A. At this point of my life I don't have any. And I don't mean to sound or be cliché, but that's the truth. I wake up take my sons to school, and I ride around selling CD's until they get out of school.

Q. So is this a pattern you plan to have forever?

Music, Kids, Sleep, Repeat?

A. Not much sleep, but I honestly don't plan on making music too much longer after my next few projects. That's honestly why I'm going so hard this year. I have to make an impact immediately!

Q. What are you going to do when you stop doing music and why you want to stop?

A. When I'm at the level of success that I set out for myself when I began making music I will then switch to building and marketing artists for BenofficialMusic. I'm a very talented artist, but I also feel like I'm a great A&R with an ear for talent and music.

Designing is a Lifestyle

DESIGNING WAS JUST A DREAM UNTIL LISA SPATES CREATED AND INNOVATED HER BRANDS SOFLUFFY ENT AND SOFLUFFY CREATIONS

by Cheraee C.

Q. What is the name of your brand(s) and how did it feel when you started your business?

A. My brand is Sofluffy Ent and Sofluffy Creations which is my kids line. It felt good to finally start it. I had been talking about it for years and one day my best friend Sharnetta Smith was just like stop talking about it and just do it so that very next day I started looking for models and just did it.

Q. How do you plan to market and advertise your brand to get a major distribution deal in stores?

A. I plan to eventually get my own website, keep doing as many fashion shows as I can, and advertise on all of the social media sites.

Q. If you were to be put in a big or small store chain what would it be and why?

A. I would love for my brand to be in Walmart because Walmart is a store that makes things affordable for families.

Q. Are you ever going to go back to making plus size clothing or is your focus mainly on kids clothing?

A. Well I never made plus size clothes. I started out recruiting models for fashion shows helping full figure women with self esteem issues and building their confidence getting them prepared for the runway and photo shoots.

Q. What is the most heartfelt thing that one of the kids you designed clothes for ever told you?

A. After a show one of the little girls that walked for me told me I was the best and that she loved my clothes and they were fun.

Q. How long does it take for you usually to design something and how do you like your surroundings when you are designing?

A. It usually takes maybe about a hour or two depends on what I'm making I specialize in distress jean looks. I like working in an environment where it's just me I like being alone when I'm in my creative zone.

Q. Did you inherit the talent to design from someone, or were you motivated by fashion in general and taught yourself the trade?

A. No I didn't inherit my talent. I just always had a love for fashion growing up. I was always getting teased about my clothes because we didn't have the things other kids had due to my mom's drug addiction. I always just fanaticized about making my own clothes. One day my good friends name Abdul on Instagram at I make clothes taught me how to basic snitch and how to make tutus and a few other tricks.

Q. If you never make it into stores what is your next step?

A. If I don't make it in a major store I will just sell my stuff on line and start a web store.

Forbes Hip Hop Cash Kings

THE FORBES HIP HOP'S WEALTHIEST ARTISTS OF 2017 IS NOW PUBLISHED

by Semaja Turner

Sean "Diddy" Combs is the highest paid rapper in Hip-Hop with an estimated $820 million and has been on the Forbes list of Hip Hop's wealthiest artists for six consecutive years. Diddy gets all of his duckets from his agreement with Diageo's Circo Vodka, his TV Network Revolt, Sean John clothing line, Bad Boy record label, Deleon tequila, and Aquahydrate alkaline water.

Jay-Z's net worth is reportedly an estimated $810 million and his Tidal streaming service is what made him the world's biggest gainer on paper.

Andre "Dr. Dre" Young's net worth is reportedly an estimated $740 million and he still has the largest single year payday ever recorded for a living musician.

Bryan "Birdman" William's net worth is $110 million since his co-record label is home to three of the world's biggest stars which is Lil Wayne, Nicki Minaj, and Drake.

Aubrey "Drake" Graham's net worth is $90 million. Besides his music endeavors he has deals with Apple, Nike, and Sprite.

ESHA I
FB:THE REAL ESHA-I
IG: @THEREALESHA_I
SOUNDCLOUD-ESHA-I AND UNDER DUB THE ALIEN

PARTY BOYS
FB: THE NEW PARTY BOYS
IG: @PARTYBOYRIO
IG: @PARTYBOYJOCLIFF
IG:@RALLY

ROYALTY GANG
RECORDS
SHOWCASE

MIC BROWN

IG:IAMMICBROWN
FB:MIC BROWN
SOUNDCLOUD: MIC BROWN

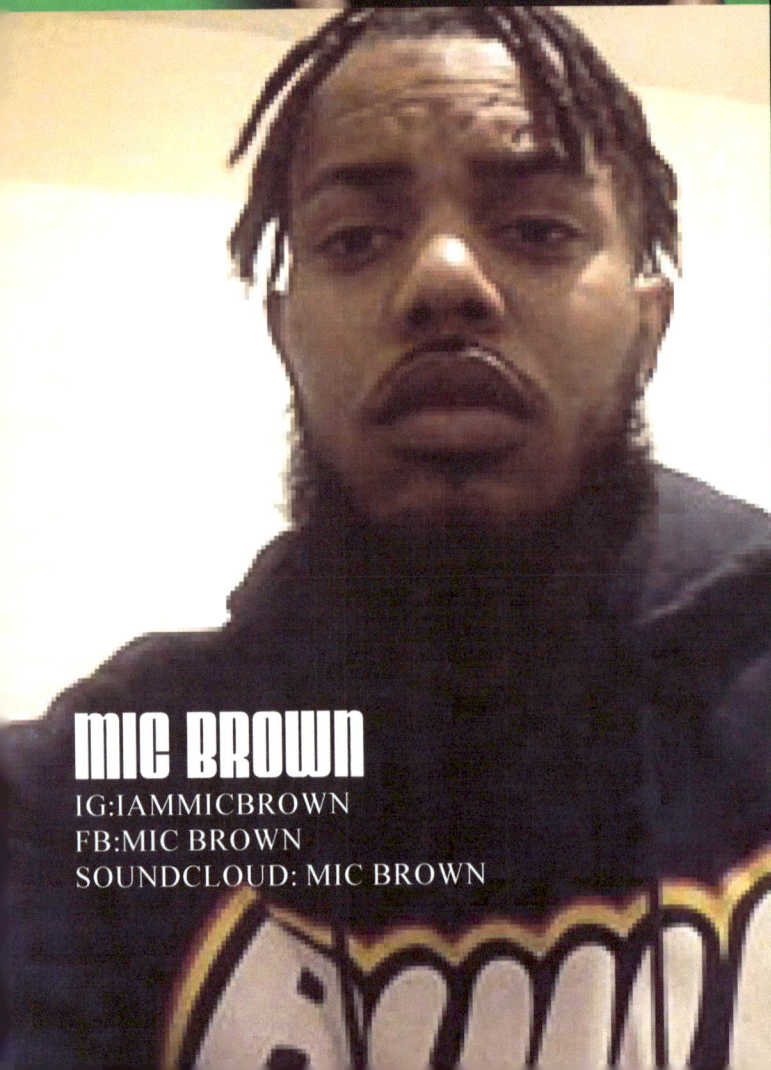

LIL DAVID RUFFIN
FB: LIL DAVID RUFFIN
IG: @LILDAVID_RUFFIN
TWITTER: @LILDAVID_RUFFIN

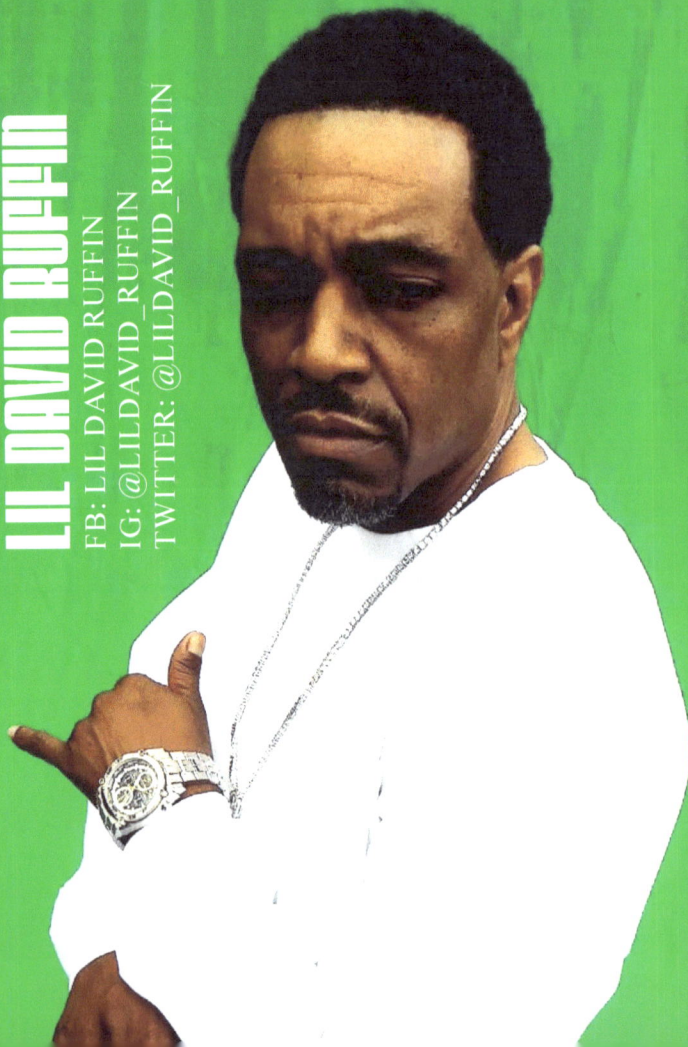

MIKE MAC

FB: MIKE MAC
IG: @_MIKEMAC
TWITTER: @EASTSIDEE_MACK
SOUND CLOUD: MIKE MAC

DESZTRO

FB: DETROITNORTHERNNA-
TIVES
IG: @DESZTRO1
YOUTUBE: DESZTRO1

AD

FB: FLYSCY DIZZLE

WOOD

FB: TJWOODHOUSE
IG: @TJWOODHOUSE

Mr. Stay Focused

NEWEST WRITER TO TEAM SDMLIVE AND CEO OF B.O.S.S STATUS /AMPTV IS READY TO LITERARY SHOWCASE HIS VIEWS TO THE WORLD

by Cheraee C.

Q. Being a well-rounded individual, which one of your crafts are you most passionate about and why?
A. Writing was the first thing I ever had a passion to do. In third grade I used to write my own Poke'mon fan fiction because I thought the concept of only 151 of the mythical creatures (at the time) was wack so I created my own and attached my own storyline.

Q. Briefly tell us about your brand B.O.S.S. Status/AMP-tv...
A. The letters B.O.S.S. stands for "Being Our Source of Success" which is a message to people to be great without permission. We use music to convey that message. We use the AMPtv brand to further amplify that message and lead by example. I have a philosophy that states "Instead of getting a foot in the door, become the door itself." We use AMPtv as a means of achieving that.

Q. If you can change anything about the entertainment industry in our city what would it be and why?
A. Erasing the parasites who prey on weaker artists that are simply attempting to showcase their craft. After awhile, it discourages artists from chasing new opportunities on fear of scam artists who make profits from the dreams they sell.

Q. Out of everything that you've been through what experience really motivated you to be in the industry?
A. I had the opportunity of songwriting for a legendary rap artist by the name of MC Breed at the age of 16. I felt like that was more than most would do in a lifetime. We were signed to the same management company, Vanglorious Entertainment which allowed me to learn the industry from the inside out.

Q. What's your vision of your career in the next five years?
A. Automation of the several companies I've started since 2012. I want my businesses operating themselves which would mean jobs for my community and more time for me to focus on my one true love of creating full time.

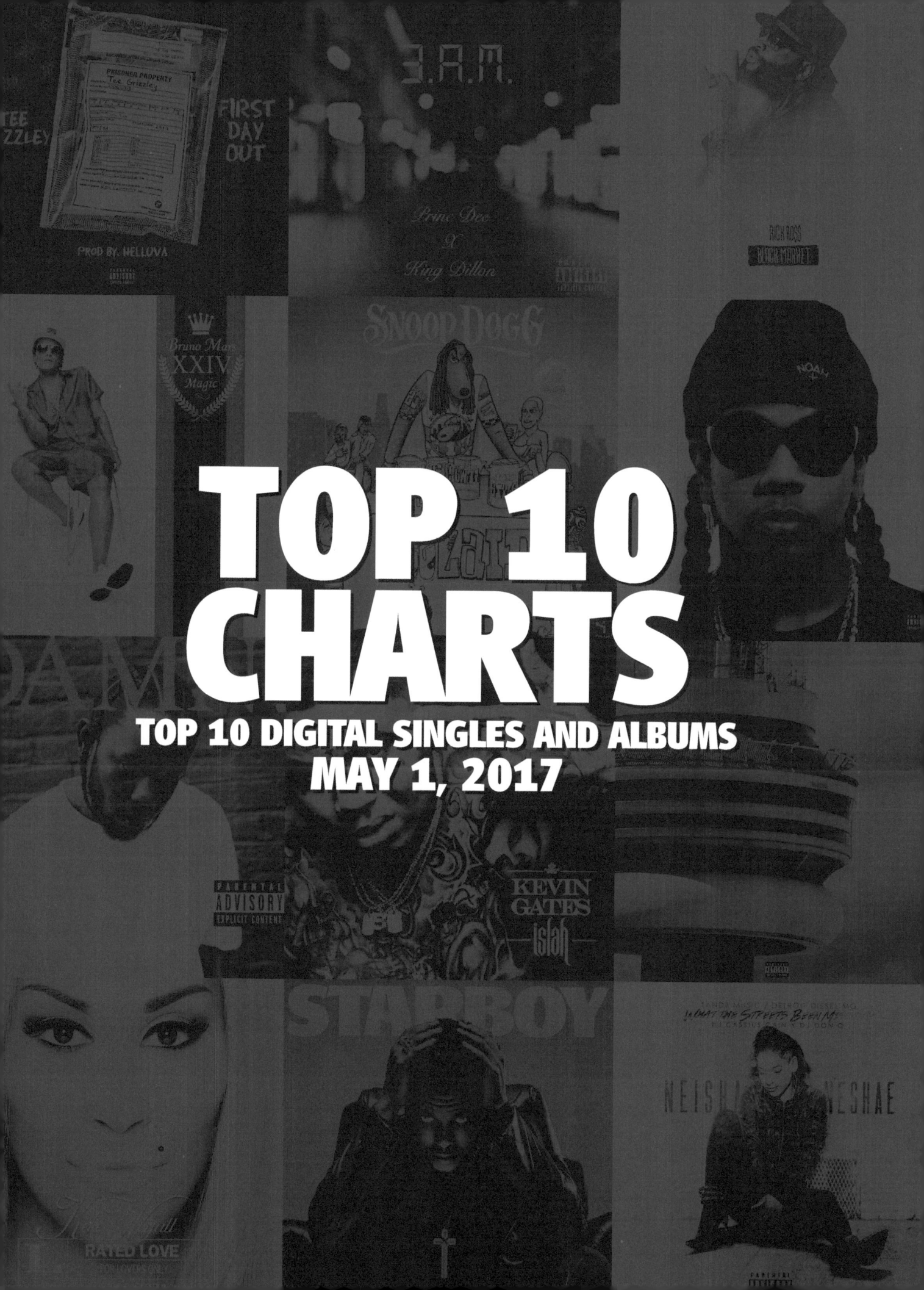

TOP 10 CHARTS

TOP 10 DIGITAL SINGLES AND ALBUMS
MAY 1, 2017

TOP 10 CHARTS

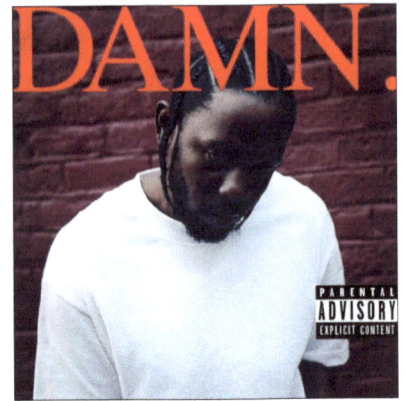

KENDRICK LAMAR RELEASED THE UNEXPECTED NEW SONG "THE HEART PART 4."

TOP 10 SINGLES
CHART OF THE MONTH

No.	Artist - Song Title
1	KENDRICK LAMAR - HUMBLE
2	BRUNO MARS - THAT'S WHAT I LIKE
3	FUTURE - MASK OFF
4	DJ KHALED - I'M THE ONE
5	BIG SEAN - JUMP OUT THE WINDOW
6	JP ONE - MILLION
7	KEON - ROLLIN WIT YOUR CHIC
8	KHALID - LOCATION
9	KYLE - ISPY FT. LIL YACHTY
10	DRAKE - PASSIONFRUIT

TOP 10 ALBUMS
CHART OF THE MONTH

No.	Artist - Album Title
1	TEE GRIZZLEY - MY MOMENT
2	RICK ROSS - BLACK MARKET
3	MIGOS - CULTURE
4	FUTURE - FUTURE
5	THE WEEKND - STARBOY
6	GUCCI MANE - THE RETURN OF EAST ATLANTA SANTA
7	THE WEEKND - STARBOY
8	BIG SEAN - I DECIDED
9	KEHLANI - SWEETSEXTSAVAGE
10	LIL UZI VERT - LIL UZI VERT VS. THE WORLD

My Moment
ARTIST: Tee Grizzley
RATING: 5

Taking the time to listen to his story was seemingly gratifying. Coming with both, a wide range of vocals, and lyrical content. Raised on the west side of Detroit, music artist Tee Grizzley presents us listeners with his debut Mixtape My Moment. My Moment provides production done mostly by the Detroit native producer Helluva, one beat from DJ Mustard and two beats from Sonny Digital. The 23 year old shares a tale of loyalty, women, the struggle and stress dealing with legal trouble and taking the opportunities that can supply a better future for himself and his family, yet dealing with the consequences and rising above it all. Tracks like "Catch It", "How Many", and "10K" vividly shows the hunger and ambition in Tee Grizzley; venting about all the money that came and went, and charging ten thousand for a feature. While tracks like "Testimony", "Day Ones" and "Side Nigga" display a mid-low tempo Tee Grizzley, allocating finely-calibrated vocals, paying respects to his peers, staying on the right path through great advice and support, and also being there for the women who tend to become lonely while in a relationships. From using his hands to amplify a tasteful beat on a table and adding a strong alluring flow for his "My Moment Intro", to listening to Tee Grizzley deliver his "Testimony", My Moment is attached with the hardships of money, trust, and respect, while staying real/honest in the city of Detroit and never switching up. The potential and talent that comes out of the city is amazing and I'm overly proud of this artist for doing a total three sixty upon his life! Dope Mixtape, Check out Tee Grizzley's debut mixtape My Moment on Spotify!

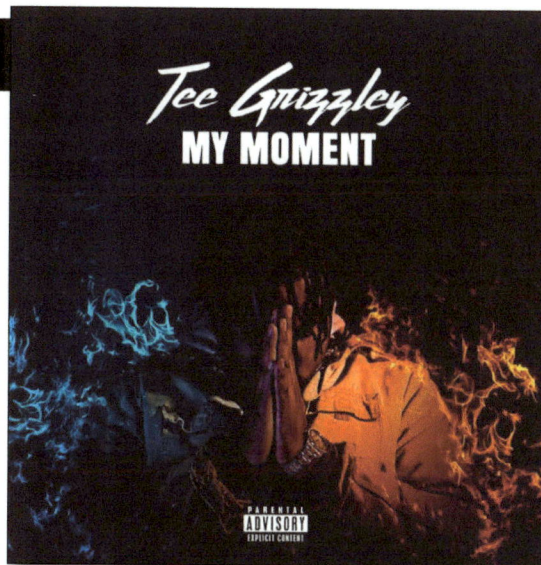

"I Know They Prayed On My Downfall(2x). On All Ten, Bitch I Stood Tall. Show These Disloyal Niggas How To Ball."

Black Market
ARTIST: Rick Ross
RATING: 4

2017 has been a big year in music already. With so much going on it was perfect timing for the biggest boss in hip hop to come out and grace us with his presence. Coming in off of the heels of the so so "Black Market" album this is the first project in a very long time that sounds like the Ricky Rozay we all love. With a classic Ross intro featuring Raphael Saadiq, and on the fifth line of the first verse we hear a Nicki Minaj shot which I know got everyone excited for this new project. Ross also gives Birdman a look in the mirror that only another executive could. He tells him just how wrong he is and how much pain he has been responsible for during the course of Cash Money Records. Ross tackles the Lil Waynesituation that has dominated music for the past few years, the fact that no one got paid what they deserved from the label and how DJ Khaled took a major loss after his stint at YMCMB. Over the course of the album there are more and more shots aimed at Birdman, and even a line in regards to Stacy Dash. He also reignites the Maybach Music series with a fifth installment featuring Dej Loaf that takes the love song route. Standouts on this record are "Idols Become Rivals", "Powers That Be" featuring Nas, & "Lamborghini Doors" featuring Meek Mill and Anthony Hamilton.This is an exciting time in music and the first time Rick Ross has utilized the new school style of album rollout and it is a total success. Ross easily outshines the various albums dropped this past weekend.

HEELS &
SKILLZ

DA TRUTH

is a beautiful model
from Detroit, MI.

instagram
@datruth101

Photography by
@barearmy

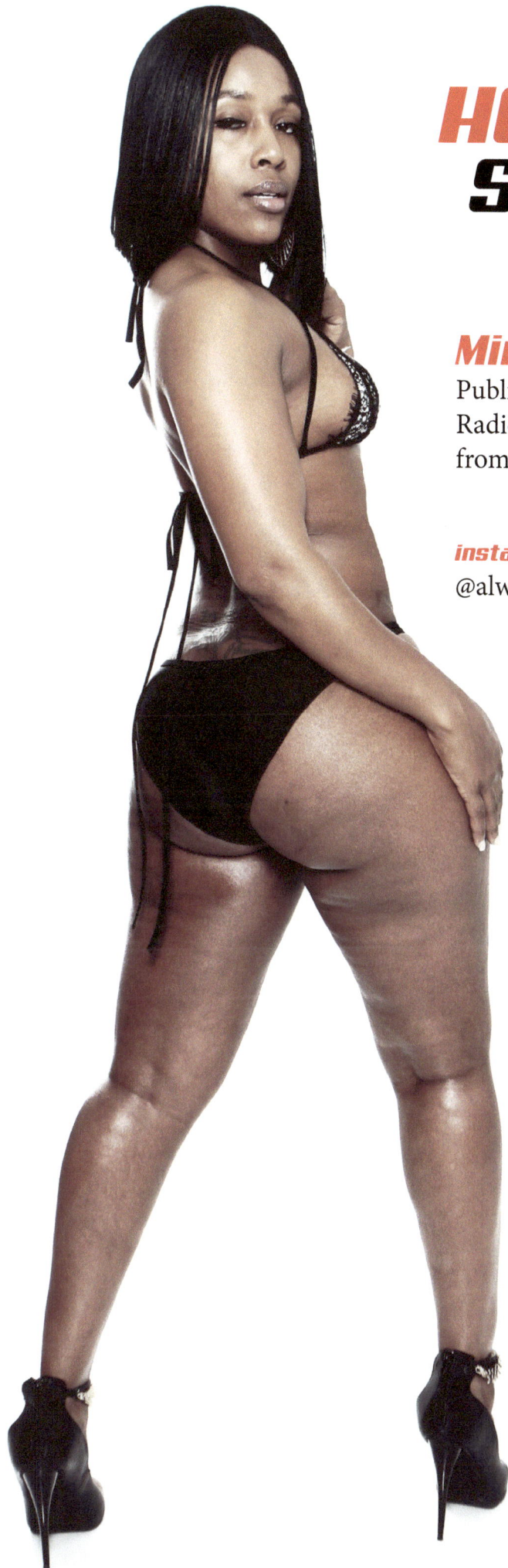

HEELS &
SKILLZ

Minyetta Bailey
Published Model and
Radio host for SDM Radio
from Detroit MI.

instagram
@alwaysmsme

Photography by
@terancedrake

HEELS & SKILLZ

Gangsta Doll

A video model in the movie True Religion from Detroit MI.

instagram
gangstadolll

Photography by
@barearmy

Cheraee's Corner
WHY DO PEOPLE TREAT THEIR BUSINESS RELATIONS NONCHALANT?
by Cheraee C.

These days in the business world, communication should be key, but it isn't. You wake up doing business with people one day, and next thing you know you never hear from that person again until they send you an invite to one of their events. What happened to having proper etiquette and respect for the person you do business with? People are so boisterous and outspoken for everything except business.

Whether you want to decline, quit, or accept a business venture, some type of communiqué should always be given whether it's a text, email, a snapchat, or etc. It's unprofessional to end good business without some type of disclosure and then turn around and expect support from them in the business world. Most people can be so much richer, but not if we fail to be business-minded.

NEXT 2 BLOW

AVA

Q. What is your biggest fear when it comes to being in the music industry?
A. My biggest fear would be letting the people who believe in me down. I feel like I have my whole family riding on this lol and so failure isn't an option for me. I gotta get in somehow.

Q. What made you start your own radio show "The Ladies Room" and who's on the show with you?
A. "The Ladies Room" Yes!! Well I've always wanted to do radio since a child so that's number 1 and for the "Ladies Room" I had a vision of a panel of women with different personalities shout out to my partners Triece Chamber (The Bag Lady) and Killa K.

Q. Describe what is the basis of the show and how can we tune in…
A. On the show we have everyday life conversations with wine just as they would if they were at home in the kitchen cooking, playing cards, having drinks. However you chop it up the ladies, but on air and worldwide so everyone can have the opportunity to be apart, able to share their views and opinions on the latest news, topics, fashion, gossip, etc.. I want it to be like therapy. We all need someone to talk too so why not tune into The Ladies Room on 7mileradio.com every Tuesday at 6PM and add it on FB to watch it live.. It gets pretty lit.

Q. As a female artist do you think it's better to base your image like Lauryn Hill, Erkyah Badu, Alicia Keys, or Nicki Minaj?
A. None of thee above… I believe you should get people familiar with you being YOU! Create your own lane… Yeah!! Those women are all awesome, but they already got them on lock… They're all known for what they're individually known for so if you try to duplicate its gonna be very obvious lol so I say create your own image… Be different.

Q. If someone was to catch you on the street, what would you be doing, and where would you be?
A. If someone was to catch me in the streets I would probably be headed to a gig with my band LIVEWIRE going to a rehearsal, a studio session, work, or promoting my single "Rare."

Q. What would you do if you couldn't do music anymore?

A. If I couldn't do music anymore I would probably focus more on my digital art, design, and illustrating. That's kind of my side hustle right now.

Q. Why do you call yourself the Princess of R&B?

A. I've been called an R&B Princess or the Princess of R&B for years and I've never really liked it because I didn't wanna be known as just an R&B artist. I do Pop and Electronic as well, but all my supporters and my team love the R&B side so now I'm just starting to embrace it.

Q. Out of all the singles you had thus far, what is your favorite single and why?

A. My favorite single right now would have to be my newest one "Daddy," which also features my brother Flawless of the Olympicks. It's a real swaggy and sexy R&B song. I'm really excited to shoot the video for it next month.

Q. What is the best and worst reaction you ever received at a show?

A. The best reaction I've had at a show was when I did a showcase out in Atlanta. They liked me so much which resulted in me winning and also they wanted me to do an encore. I've never experienced that before so that was like a real big thing for me. I've never really had a bad reaction at a show. However, there were a few times when I felt like my performances could've been way better. I can be really hard on myself.

Q. Is it anything you've done in the music industry you regret? Why or why not?

A. One major thing I regret is not being consistent and giving up on my music career. I'm a mom so trying to go after my dreams while working a regular job back then, years ago, was stressful. Now I'm more strong minded and more ambitious. I see the bigger picture.

Q. If it's one thing you could tell the world about yourself that they don't know what would it be?

A. I'm very passionate about art, I draw a lot. I've been doing it since kindergarten. I love the freedom of creating when I draw, sketch, or even paint, and bringing my imagination to life.

NEXT 2 BLOW

SHAWNY

SNAP SHOTS

Email Your Snap Shots to
snapshots@sdmlive.com

5DS PRODUCTIONS®
THE PRINT MEDIA CENTER.

PRINT

DIGITAL & PRESS RUN PRICE LIST

BUSINESS CARD 2x3.5 INCHES		TRIFOLD BROCHURE 8.5x11 INCHES		POSTCARDS 4x6 INCHES	
100	$10	250	$150	250	$50
500	$20	500	$180	500	$55
1000	$30	1000	$230	1000	$65
5000	$100	5000	$350	5000	$130
10000	$170	10000	$680	10000	$250

**FLYERS - BROCHURES - BANNERS - BUSINESS CARDS - CD INSERTS
CALENDARS - EVENT TICKETS - POSTCARDS - POSTERS
YARD SIGNS - AND MUCH MORE**

DIGITAL & PRESS RUN PRINTING

FAST TURN AROUND PRINTING

GET FREE SHIPPING ON ALL ORDERS

YOU SAVE MONEY WHEN YOU PRINT AT
WWW.THEPRINTMEDIACENTER.COM
24/7 ONLINE ORDERING. CALL US NOW 1.888.718.2999

Urban Fiction, Spiritual, Motivation and more.
Order a book from Mocy Publishing today and receive FREE shipping.

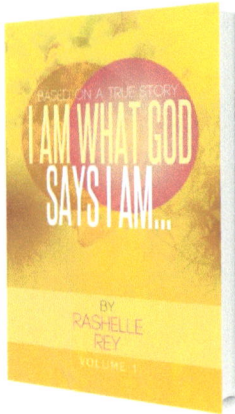

I Am What God Says I Am...
By Rashelle Rey

Item #: IAWGS29
Price: $9.99

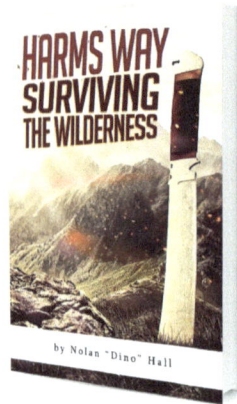

Harm's Way
By Nolan "Dino" Hall

Item #: HWS821
Price: $15.99

The Shadiest Mission Ever
By Cheraee C.

Item #: TSME28
Price: $12.99

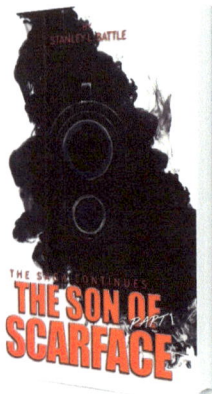

The Son Of Scarface – Part 1
By Stanley L. Battle

Item #: TSOS01
Price: $12.99

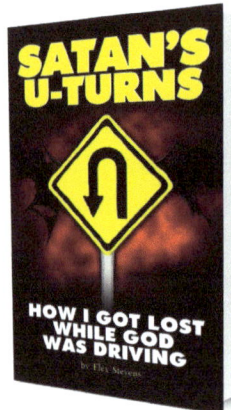

Satan's U-Turns
By Flex Stevens

Item #: SUT382
Price: $9.99

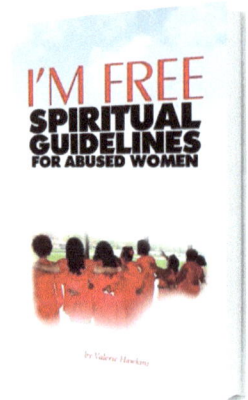

I'm Free
By Valerie Hawkins

Item #: IFTSG82
Price: $14.99

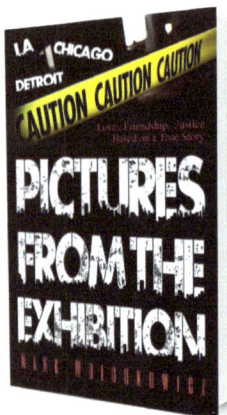

Pictures From The Exhibition
By Mark Wolodkowicz

Item #: PFAE292
Price: $15.99

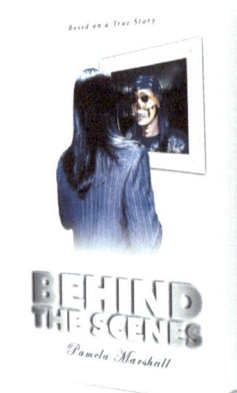

Behind The Scenes
By Pamela Marshall

Item #: BTS721
Price: $15.99

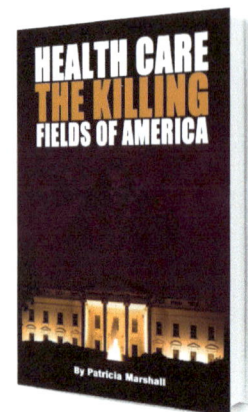

Health Care
By Patricia Marshall

Item #: HCTABF2
Price: $17.99

www.mocypublishing.com
order online and receive FREE shipping. Limit time offer.

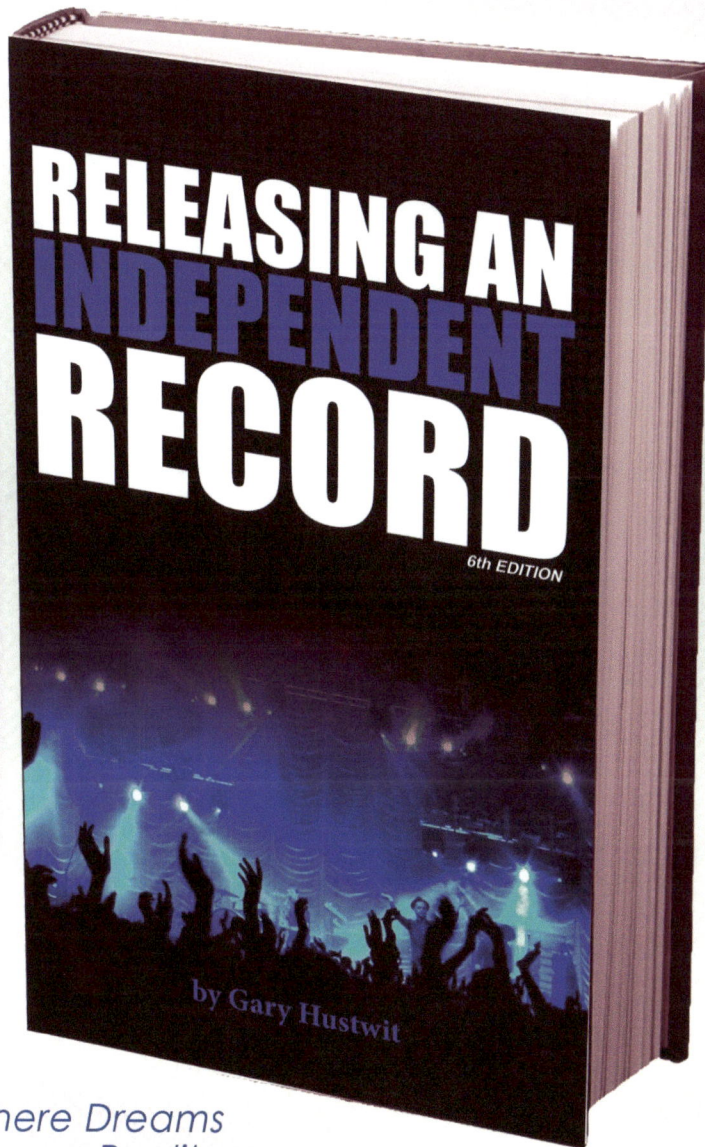

FinDDU
Fashion.com

CATERING TO THE EVERYDAY WOMAN.

DRESS LINGERIE BEZZLE
SWIM WEAR CORSETS
PLUS SIZES GOWNS

WWW.FINDDUFASHION.COM

REAL MUSIC. REAL ENTERTAINMENT.®

SDM LIVE

ISSUE 12

Also
PHILLY FAL
7MILE
RADIO
NO'EL
SNYDER
SARAH
APPLEB
LASURIA
"KANDI"
ALLMAN

NEW
KING DILLON
EXCLUSIVE P DOT

CHARLIE B. KEYZ
PUTTING IN MAJOR
LEGWORK IN THE
INDUSTRY

WWW.SDMLIVE.COM

TOYSOULJA
LAGOON
THE NEWEST
MEMBER OF
TEAM MONEY
HUNGRY

THE ALL NEW STYLE OF MAGAZINE-BOOKS

SDM LIVE ®